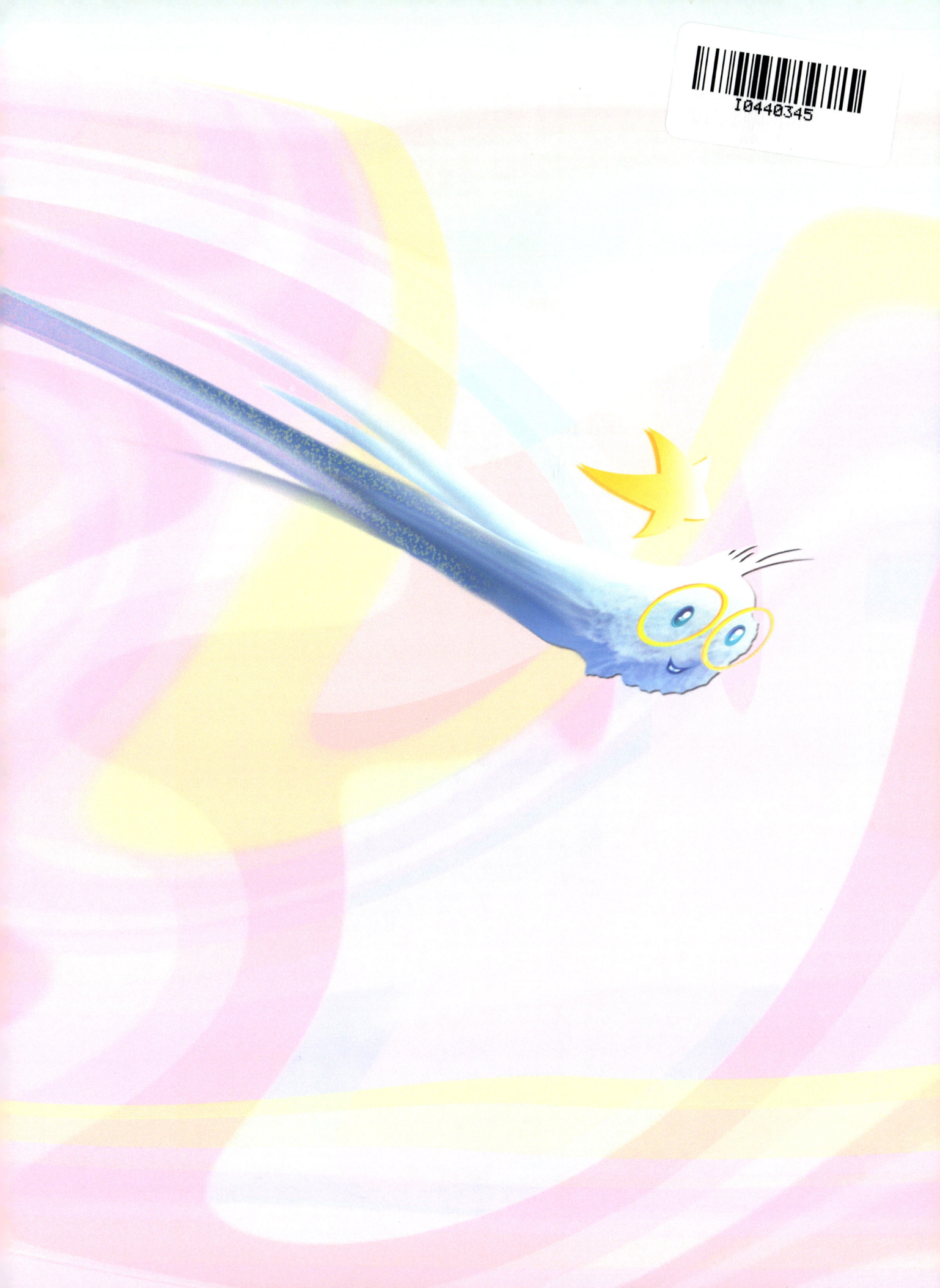

This book would not have been possible
without the love, encouragement and
support of my wife, Jan.

This book is dedicated to my daughter, Lindsey, and my grandson, Thomas.

Thomas surrounds us every day, floating on heavenly clouds.

The story was born many years ago on the back porch of our country home, one summer eve with Lindsey on my knee. There, we shared home-grown tales of characters like Ronnie the Rain Cloud. Those were the most precious moments of my life.

Ronnie
the Rain Cloud

WRITTEN BY
ROBERT BRADSHAW

ILLUSTRATED BY
ARON ROOK

Charles Bruce Foundation
Carlisle, Pennsylvania

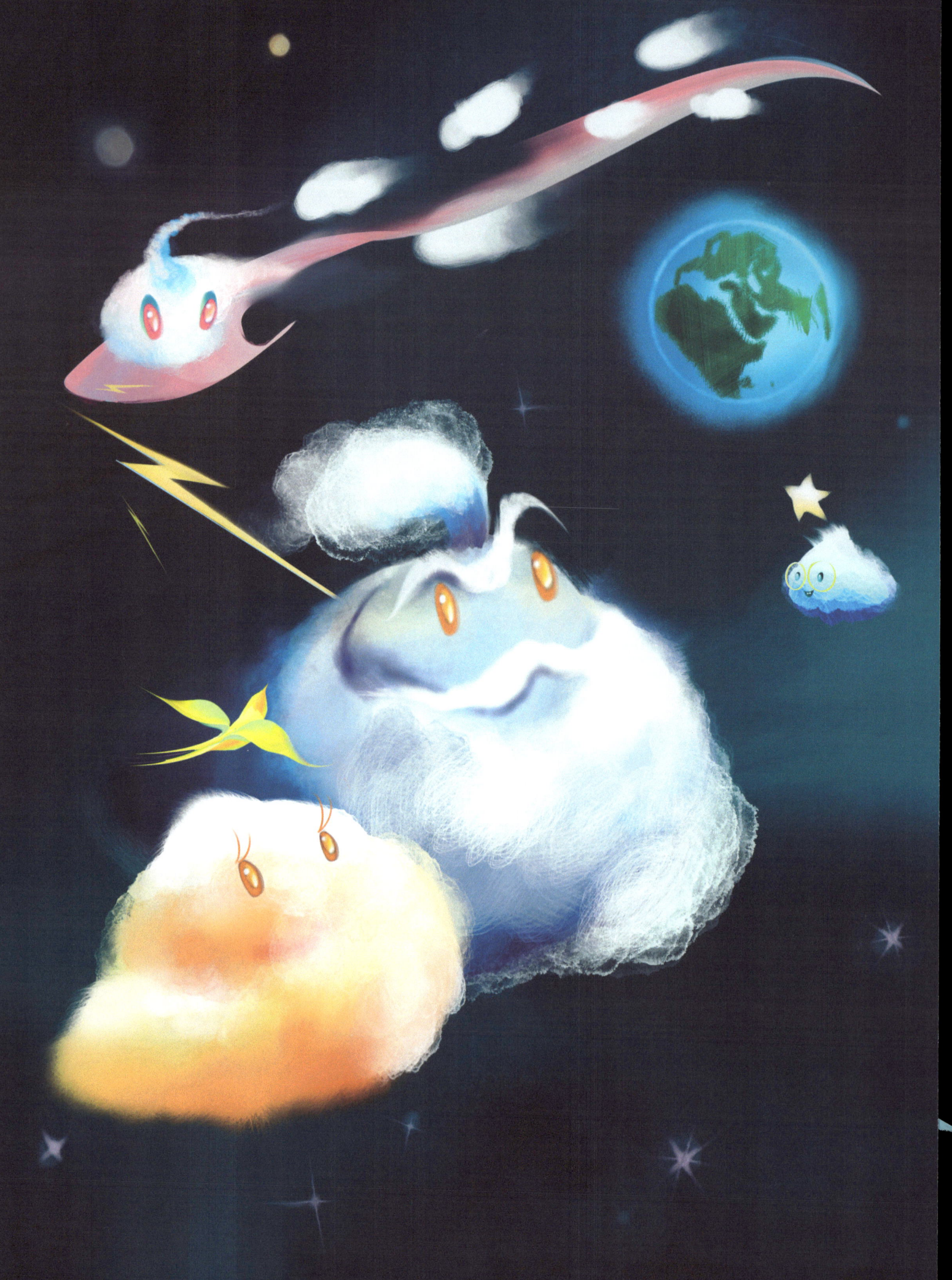

Little Ronnie Rain Cloud beamed with joy. His parents told him the good news. Ronnie was finally old enough. For the first time, Ronnie would join the Cloud Family. Together, they would float through the sky. They would travel around the world.

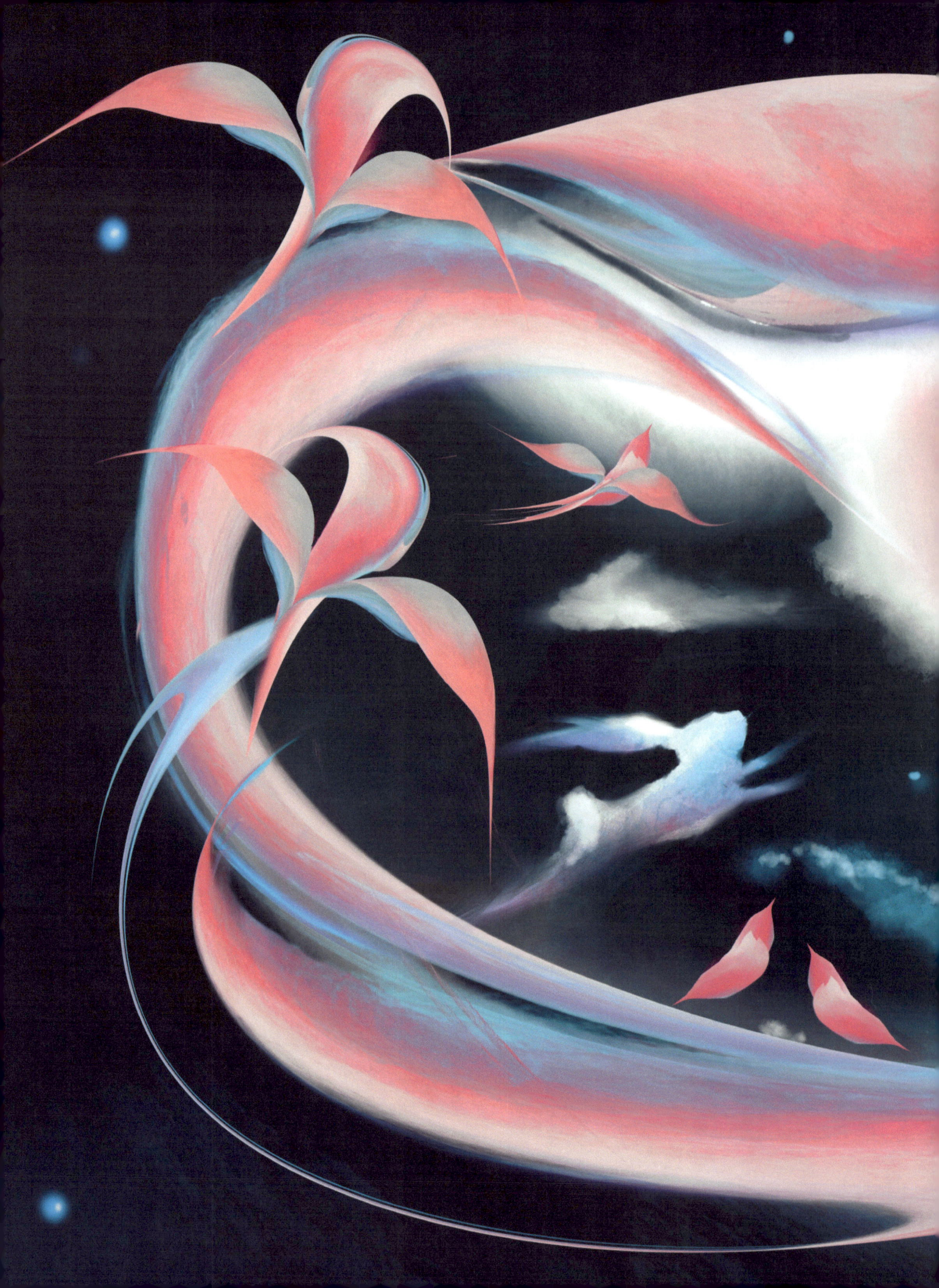

Ronnie's sister told him about the wonderful places they would see. Ronnie learned about the important work his cloud family might do. "Clouds bring rain to the world. Rain is important to the plants, animals and people."

"Rain becomes water for plants and animals to drink. Water gathers in rivers and streams where fish swim. Water helps trees grow."

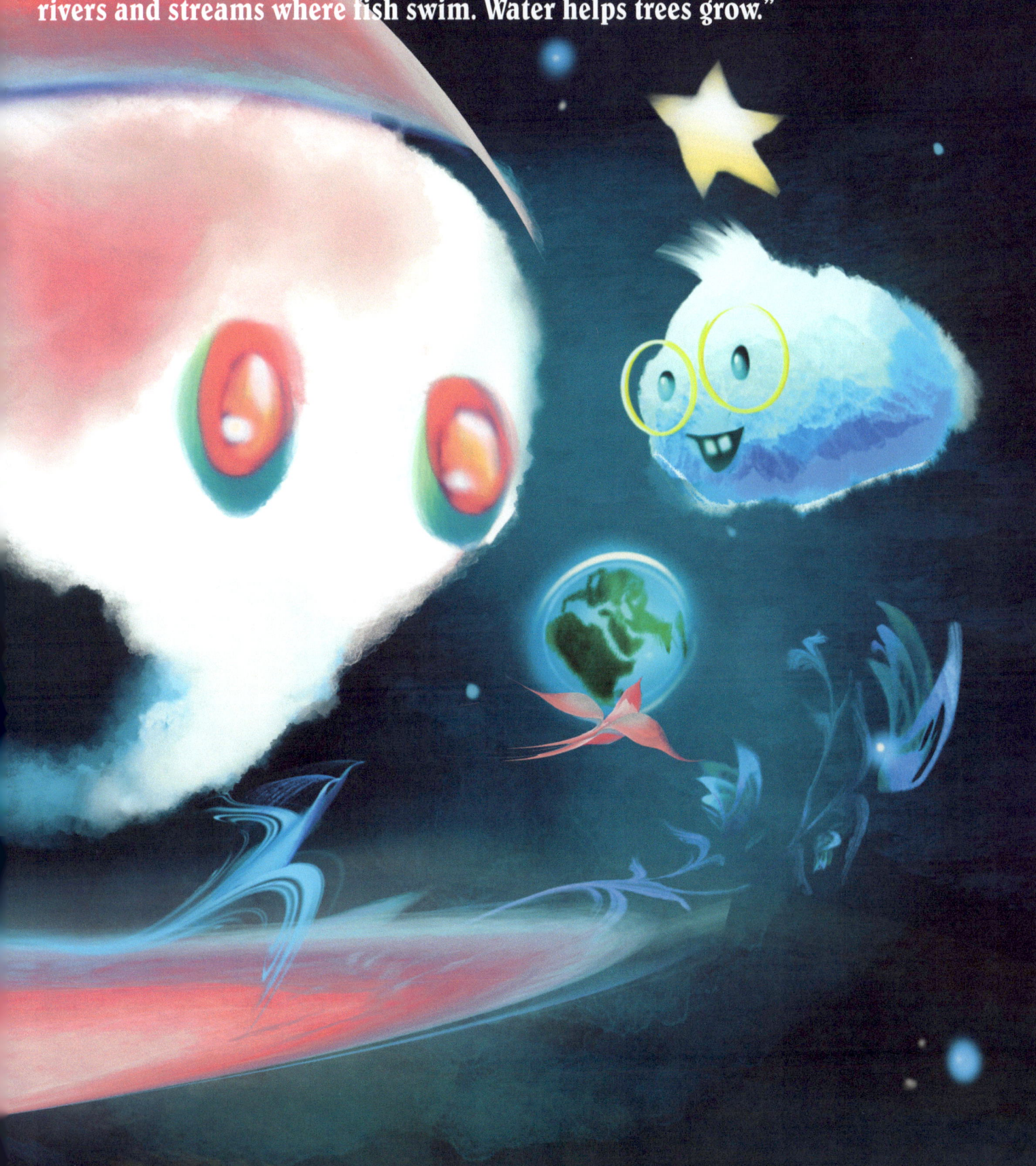

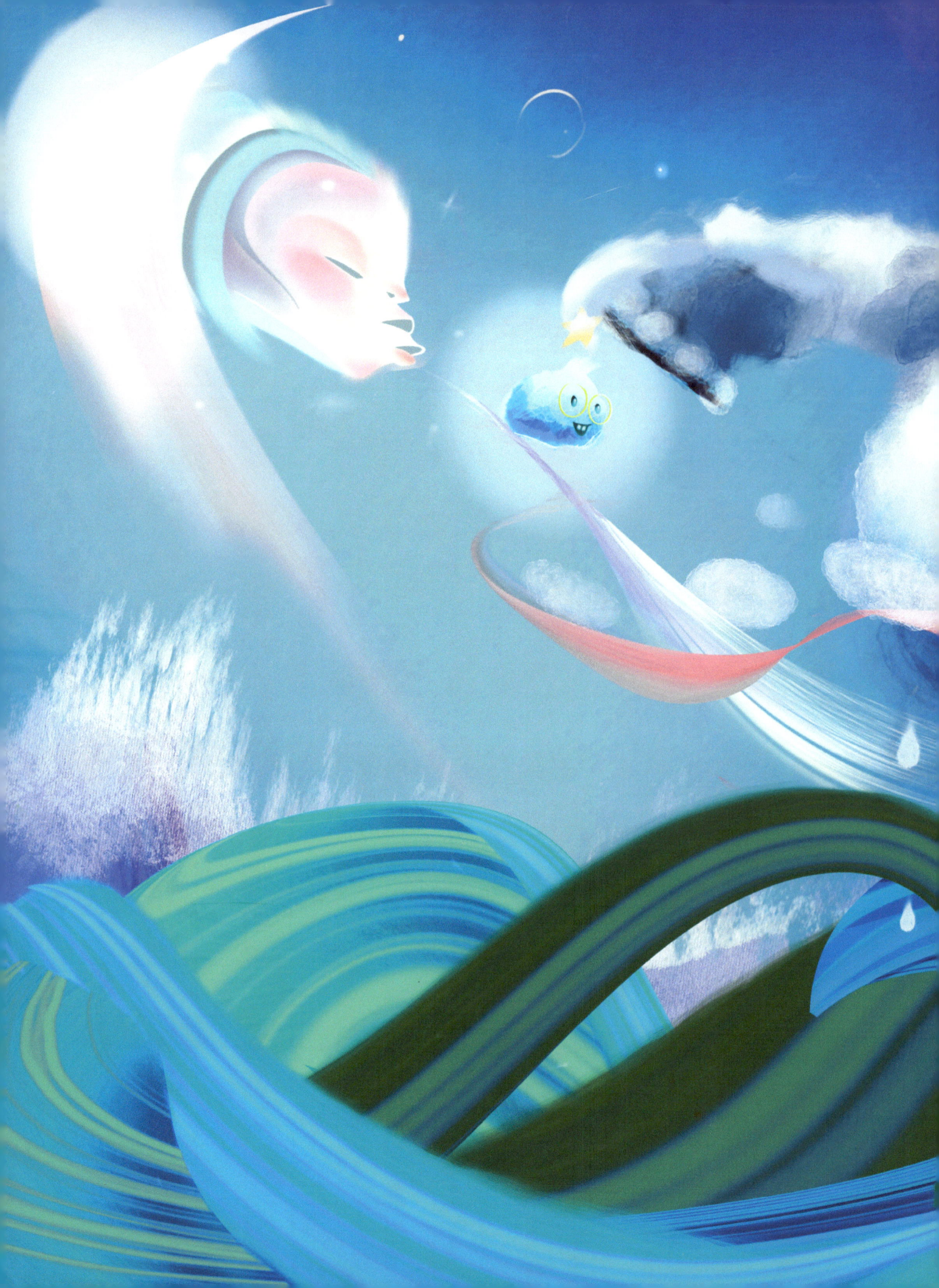

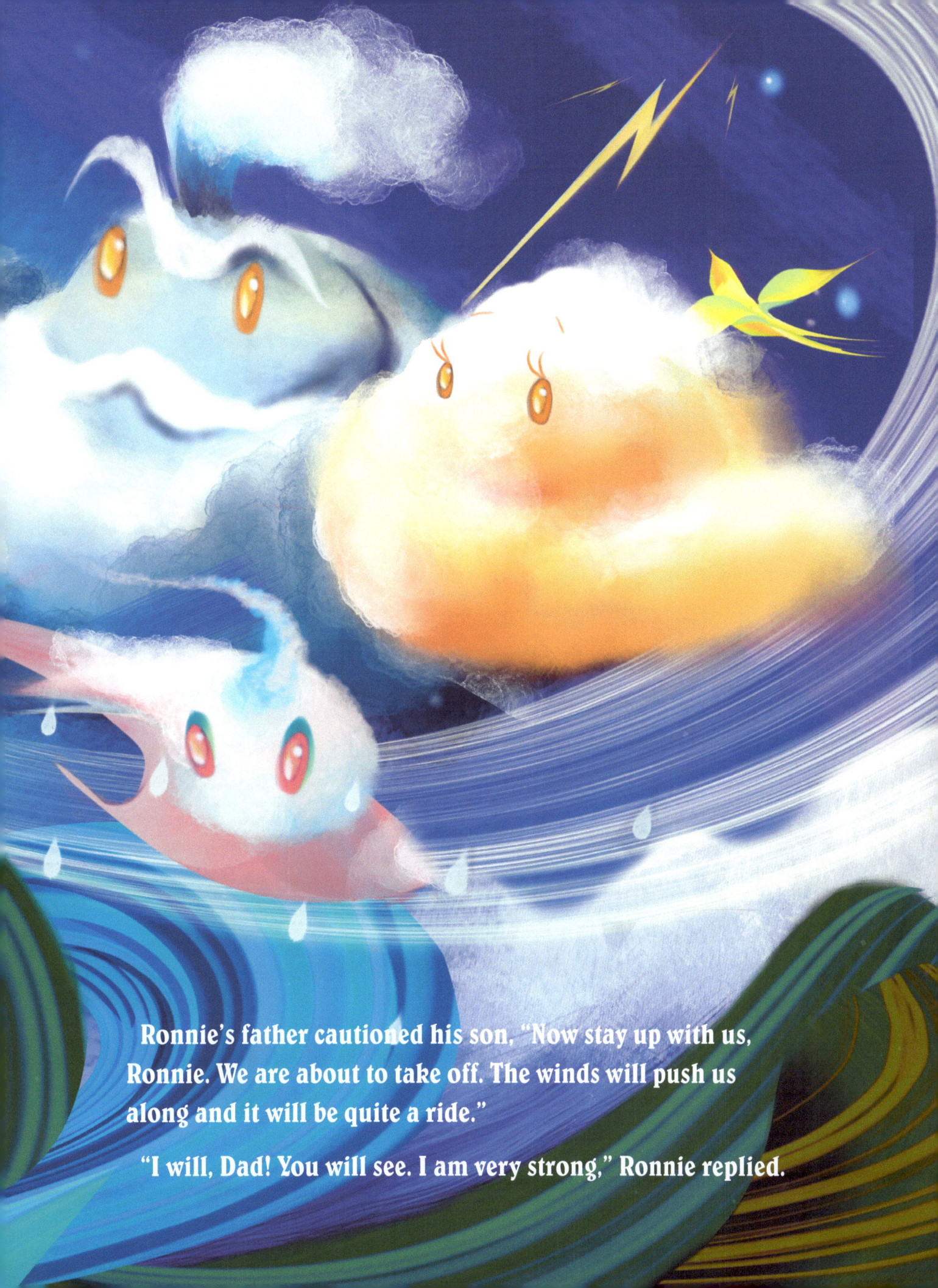

Ronnie's father cautioned his son, "Now stay up with us, Ronnie. We are about to take off. The winds will push us along and it will be quite a ride."

"I will, Dad! You will see. I am very strong," Ronnie replied.

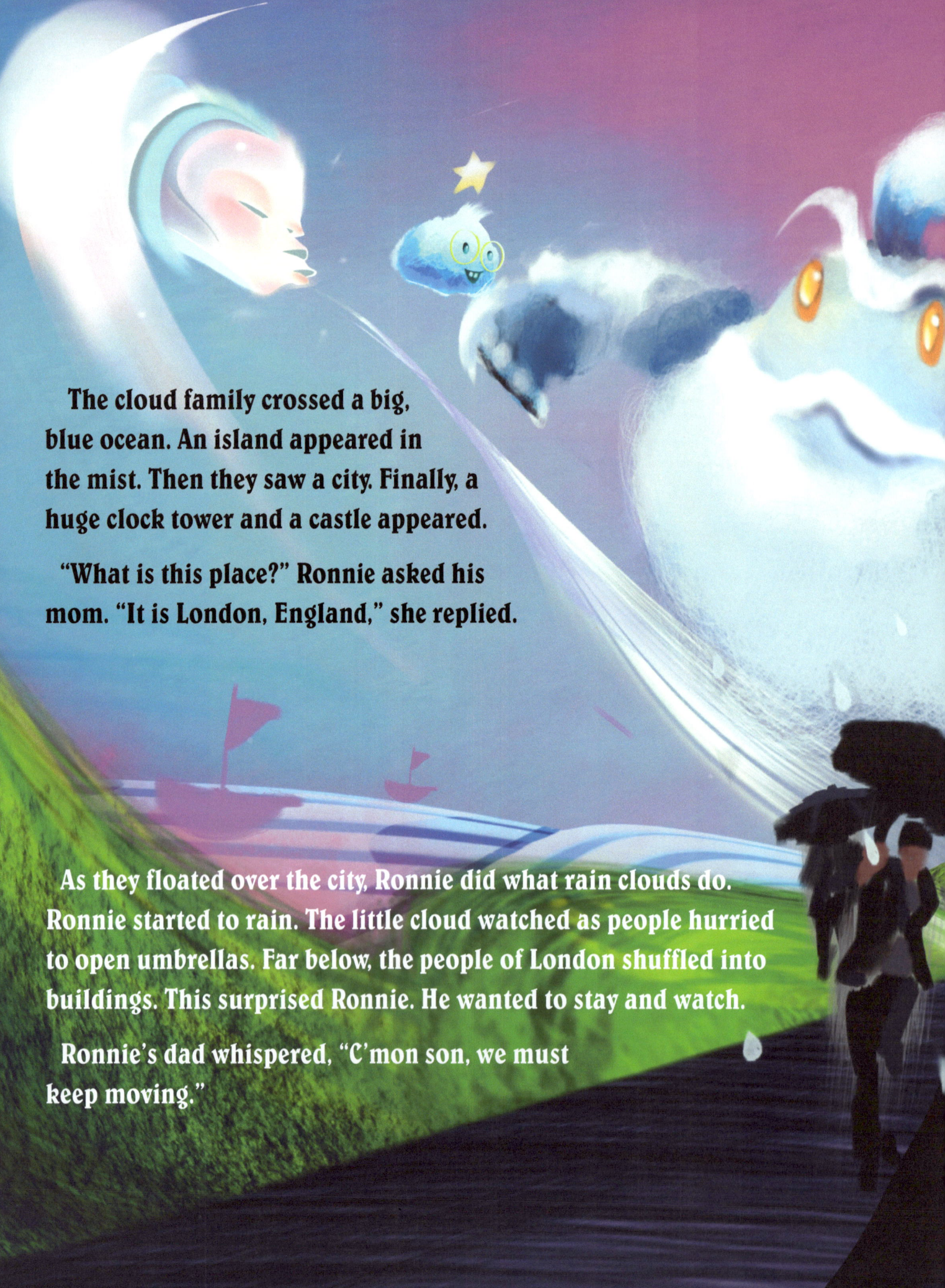

The cloud family crossed a big, blue ocean. An island appeared in the mist. Then they saw a city. Finally, a huge clock tower and a castle appeared.

"What is this place?" Ronnie asked his mom. "It is London, England," she replied.

As they floated over the city, Ronnie did what rain clouds do. Ronnie started to rain. The little cloud watched as people hurried to open umbrellas. Far below, the people of London shuffled into buildings. This surprised Ronnie. He wanted to stay and watch.

Ronnie's dad whispered, "C'mon son, we must keep moving."

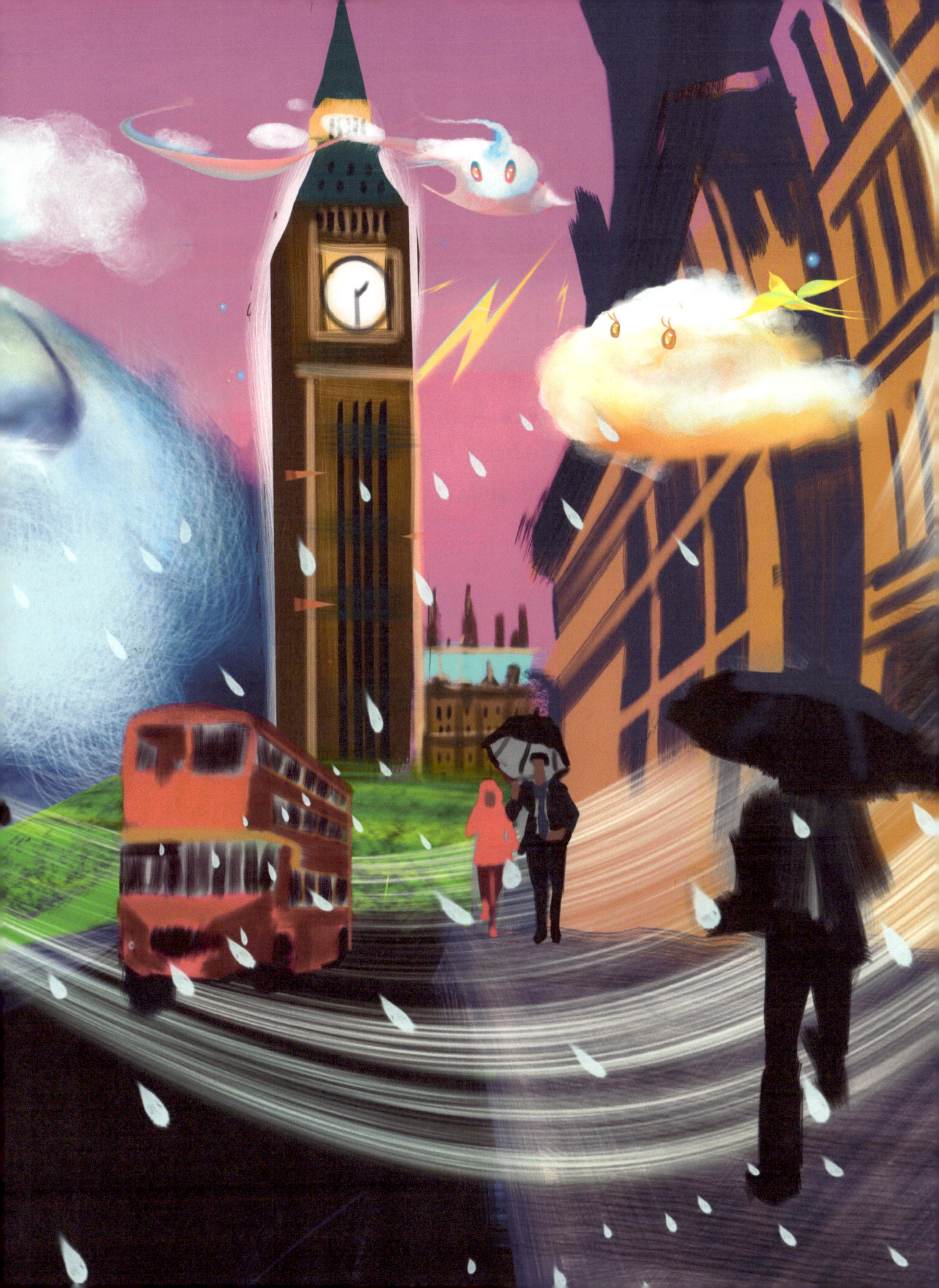

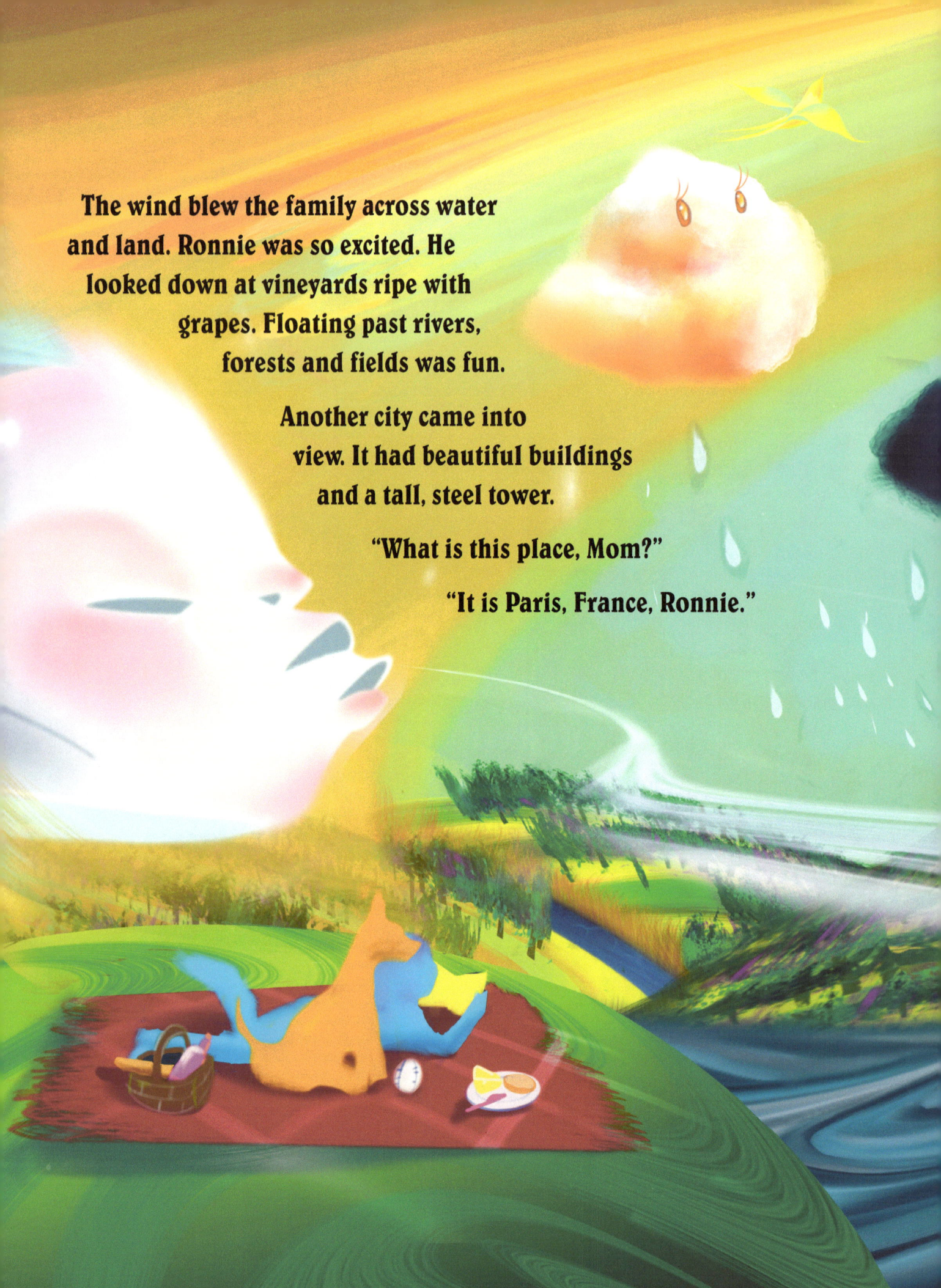

The wind blew the family across water and land. Ronnie was so excited. He looked down at vineyards ripe with grapes. Floating past rivers, forests and fields was fun.

Another city came into view. It had beautiful buildings and a tall, steel tower.

"What is this place, Mom?"

"It is Paris, France, Ronnie."

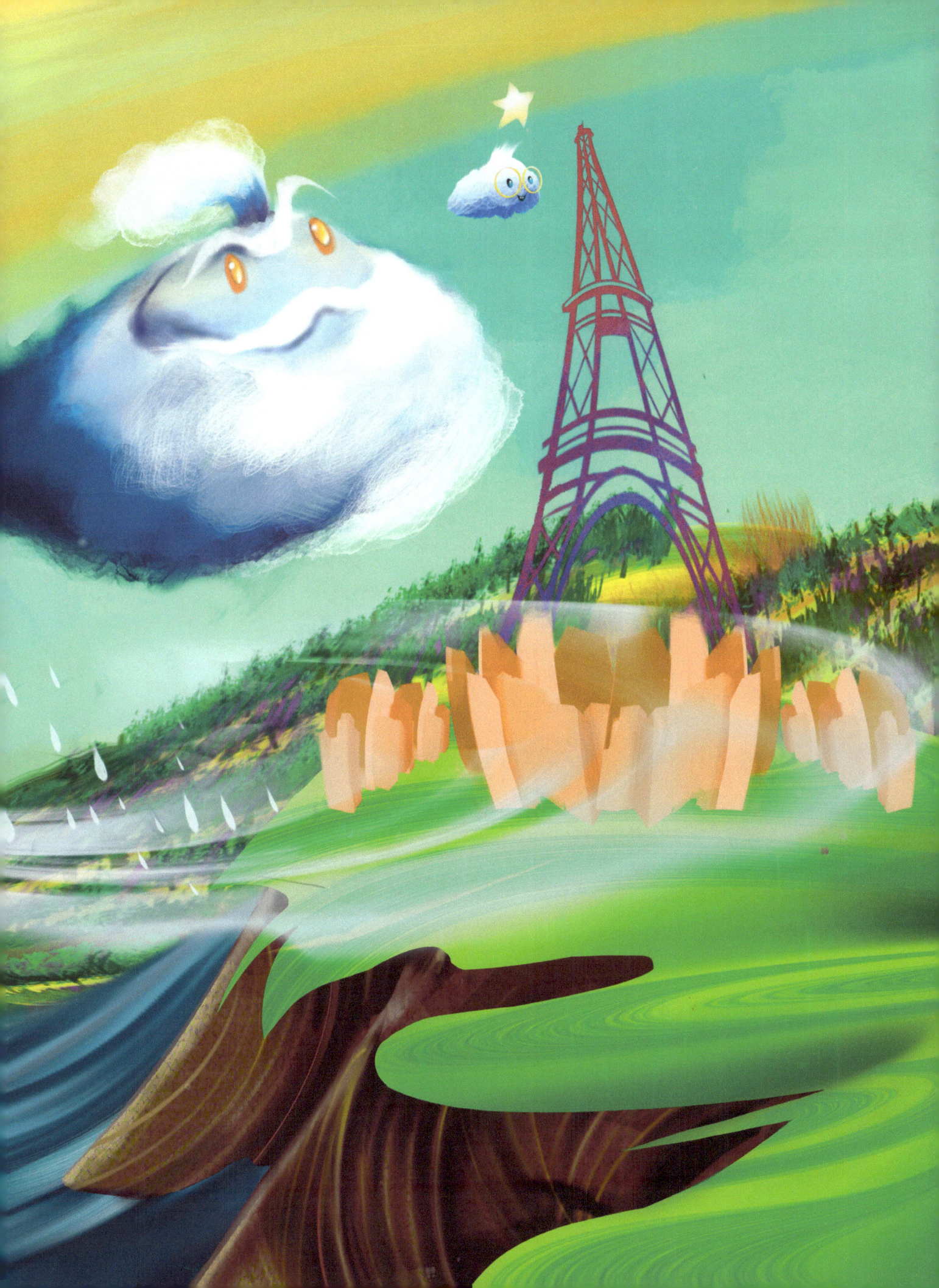

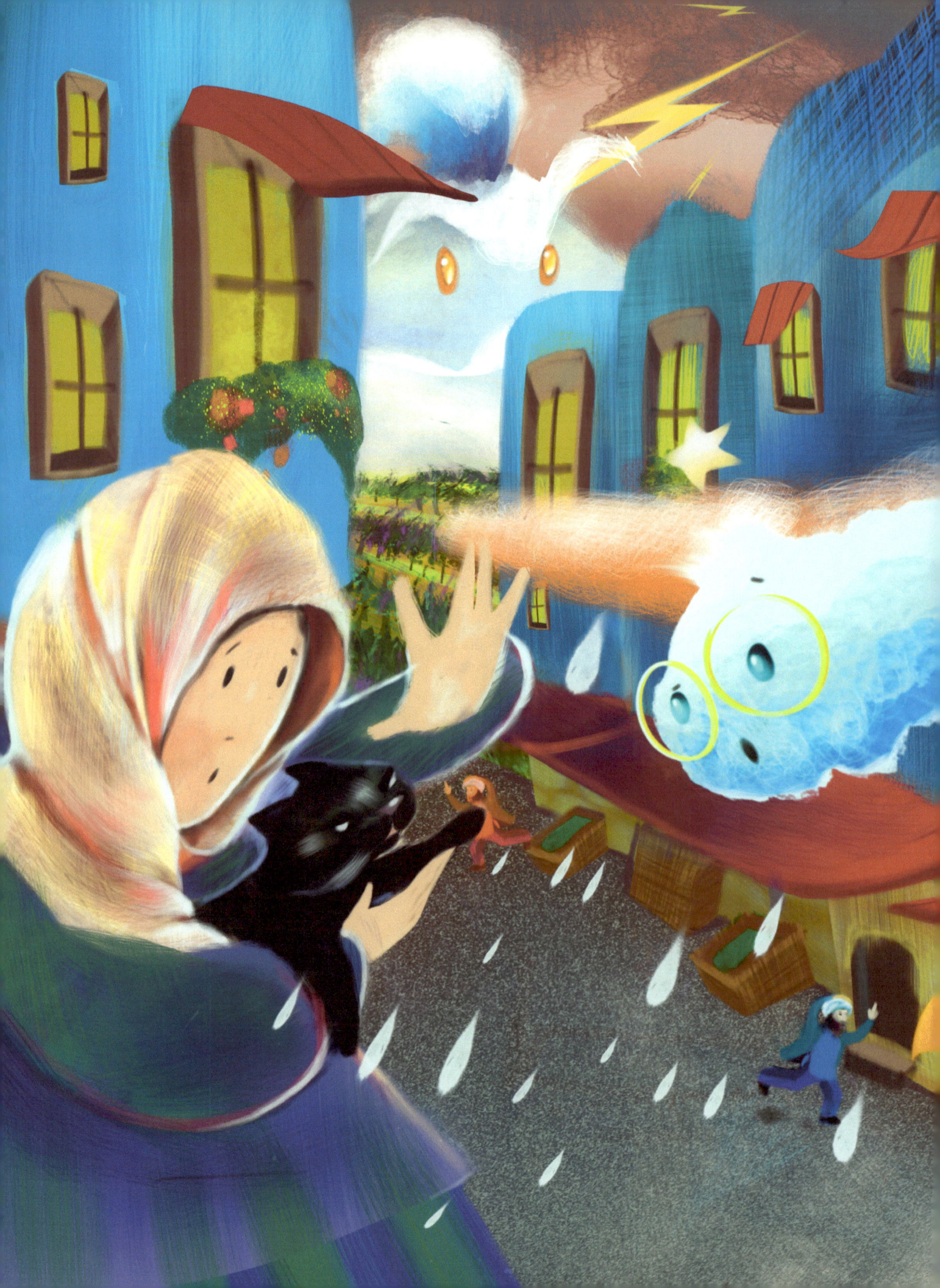

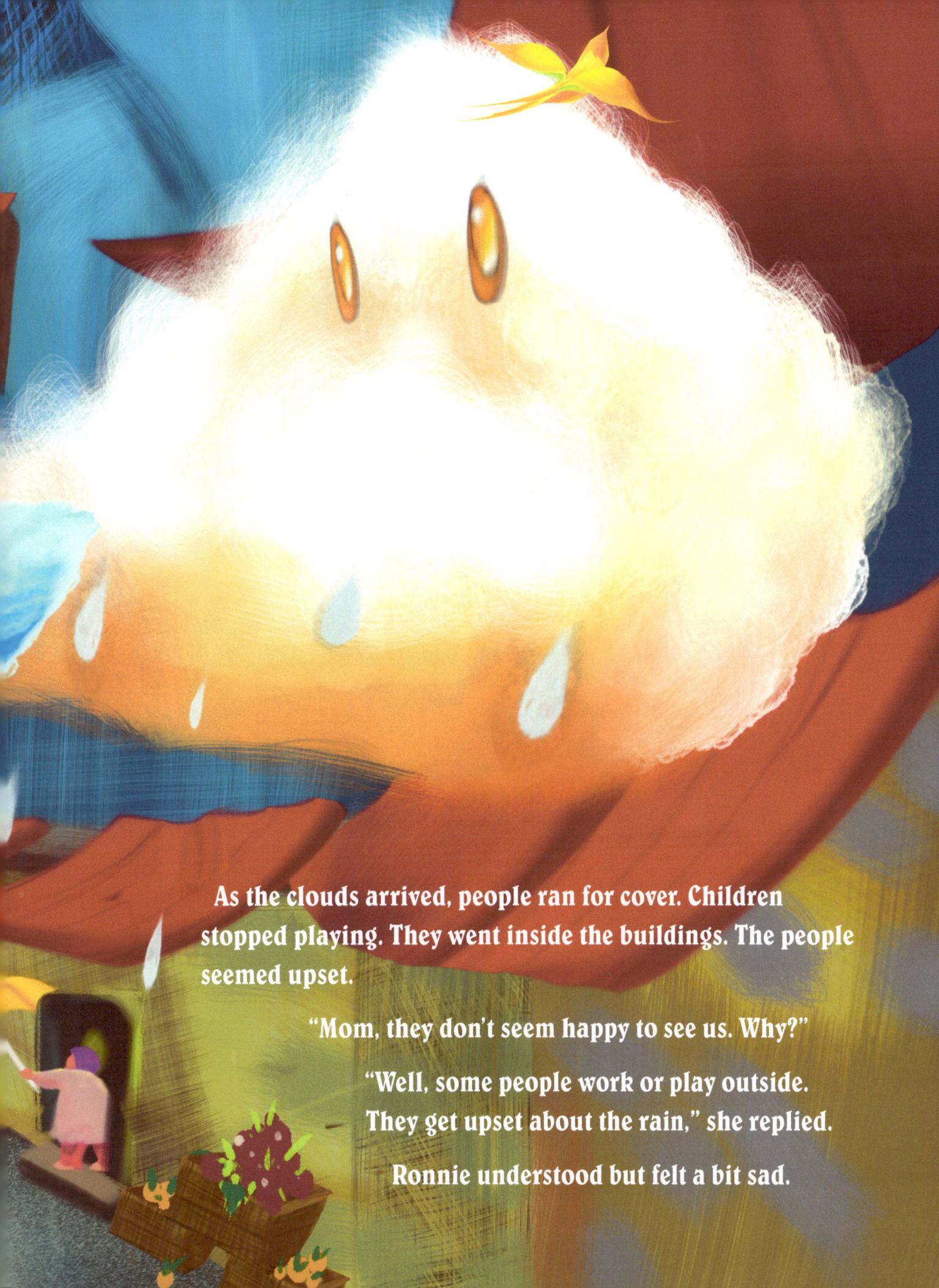

As the clouds arrived, people ran for cover. Children stopped playing. They went inside the buildings. The people seemed upset.

"Mom, they don't seem happy to see us. Why?"

"Well, some people work or play outside. They get upset about the rain," she replied.

Ronnie understood but felt a bit sad.

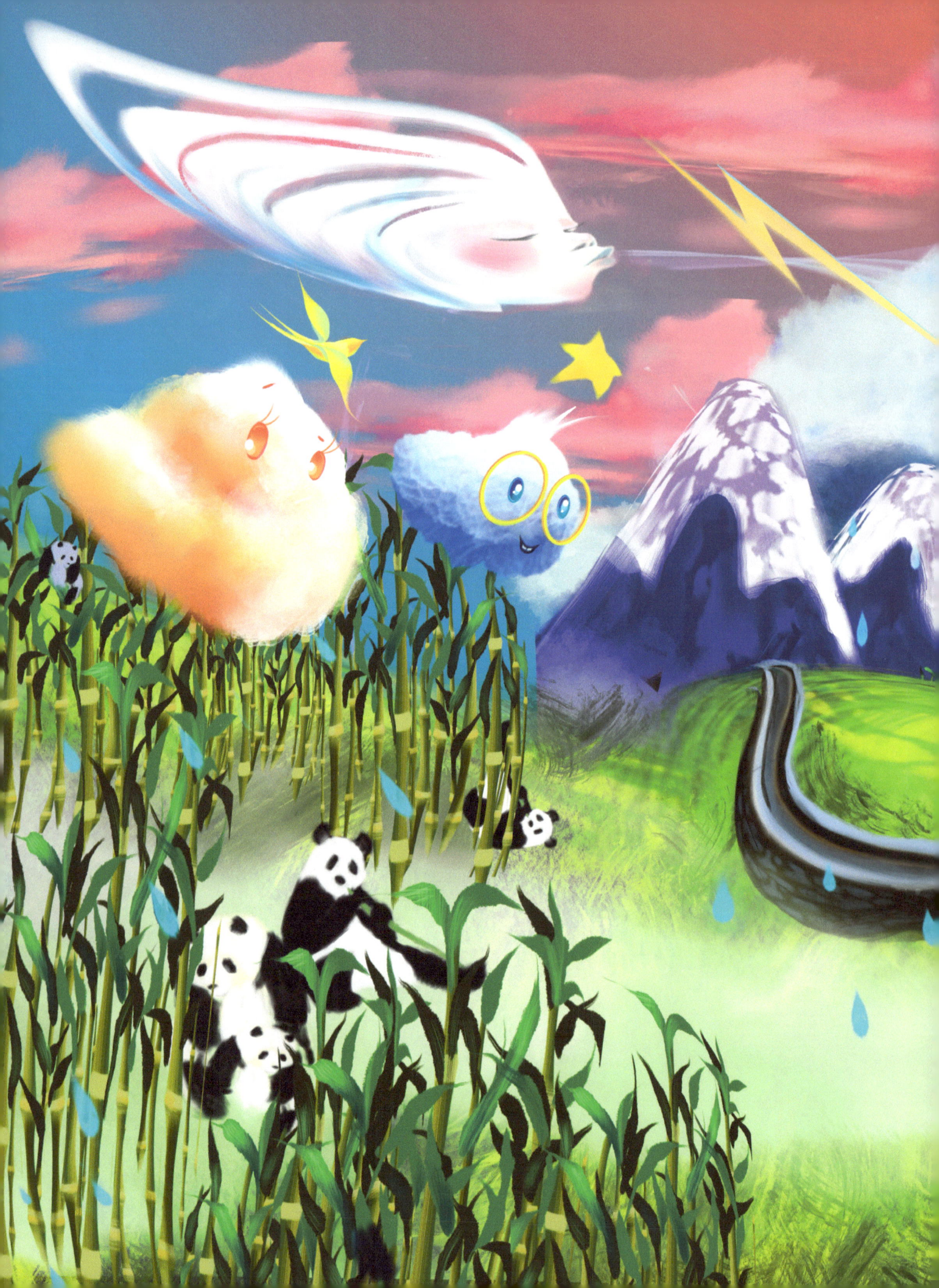

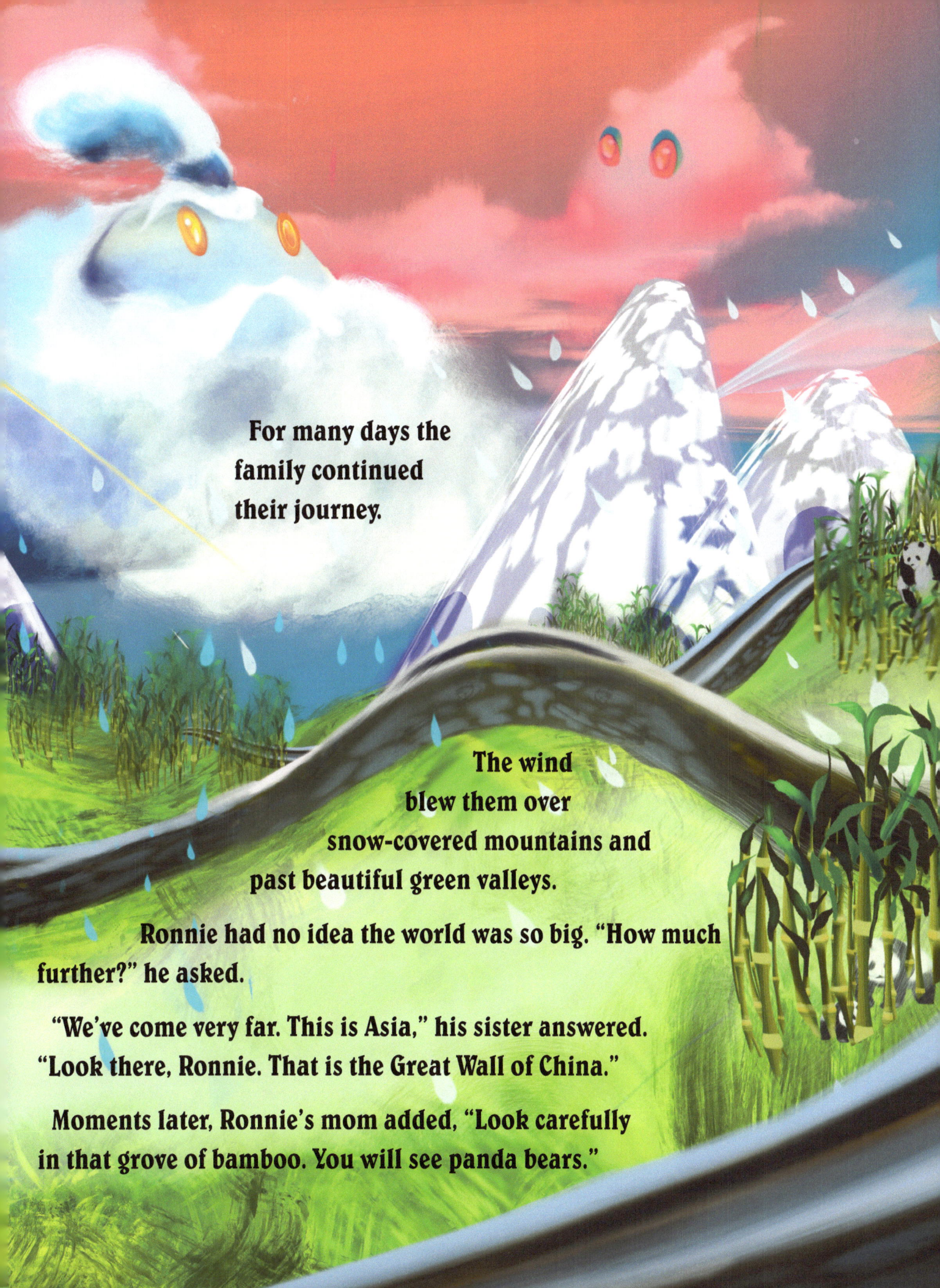

For many days the
family continued
their journey.

The wind
blew them over
snow-covered mountains and
past beautiful green valleys.

Ronnie had no idea the world was so big. "How much
further?" he asked.

"We've come very far. This is Asia," his sister answered.
"Look there, Ronnie. That is the Great Wall of China."

Moments later, Ronnie's mom added, "Look carefully
in that grove of bamboo. You will see panda bears."

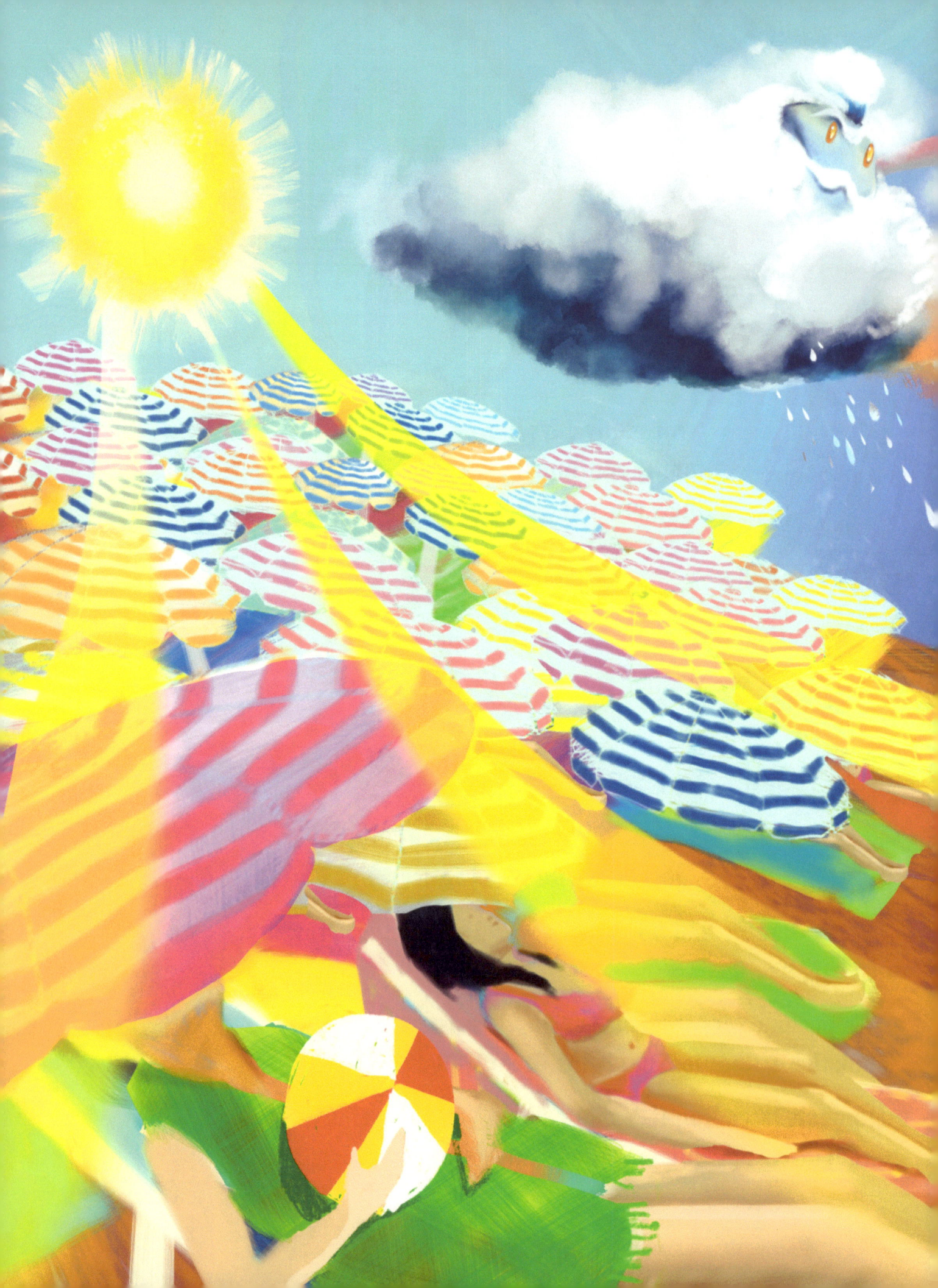

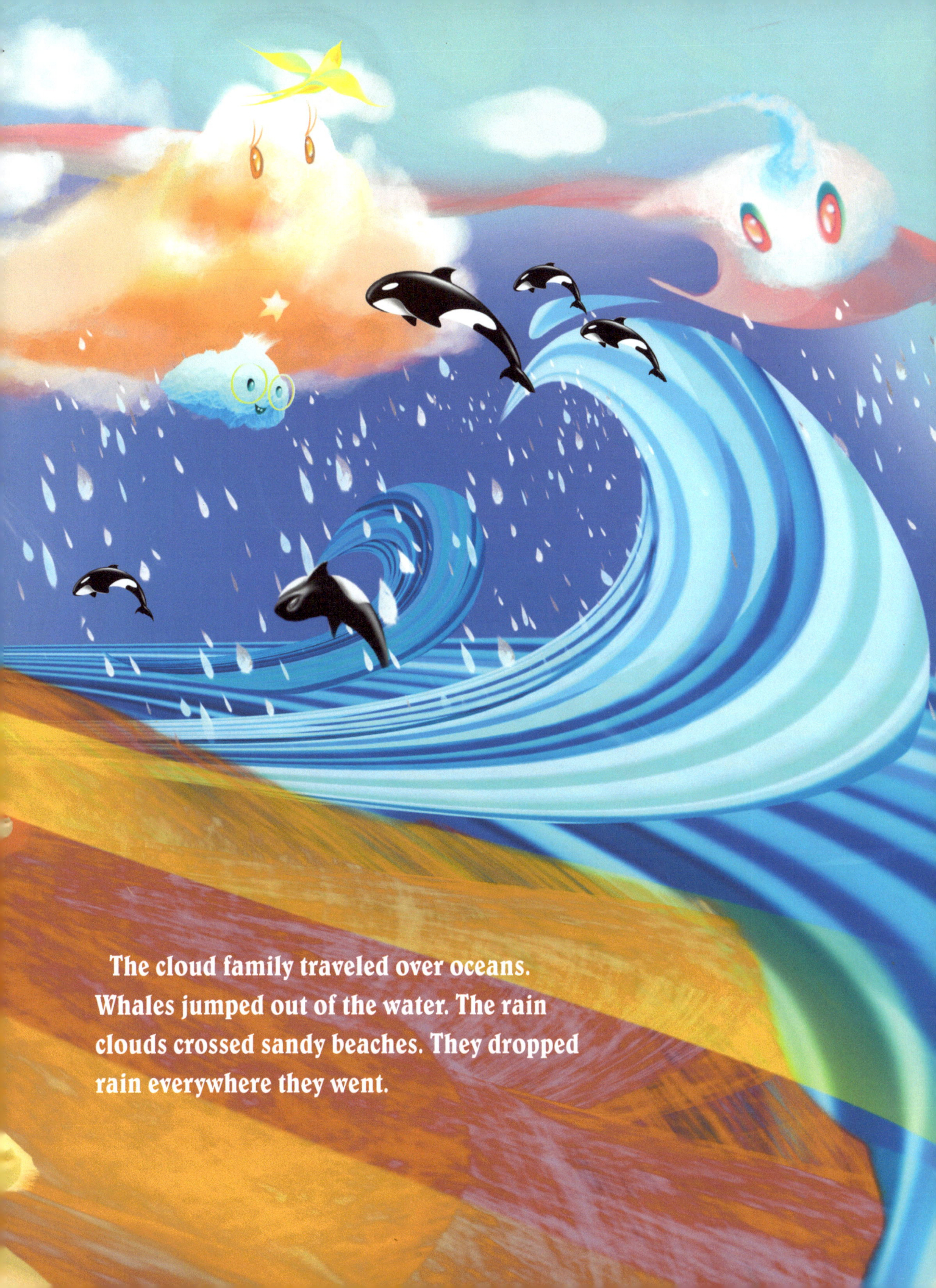

The cloud family traveled over oceans. Whales jumped out of the water. The rain clouds crossed sandy beaches. They dropped rain everywhere they went.

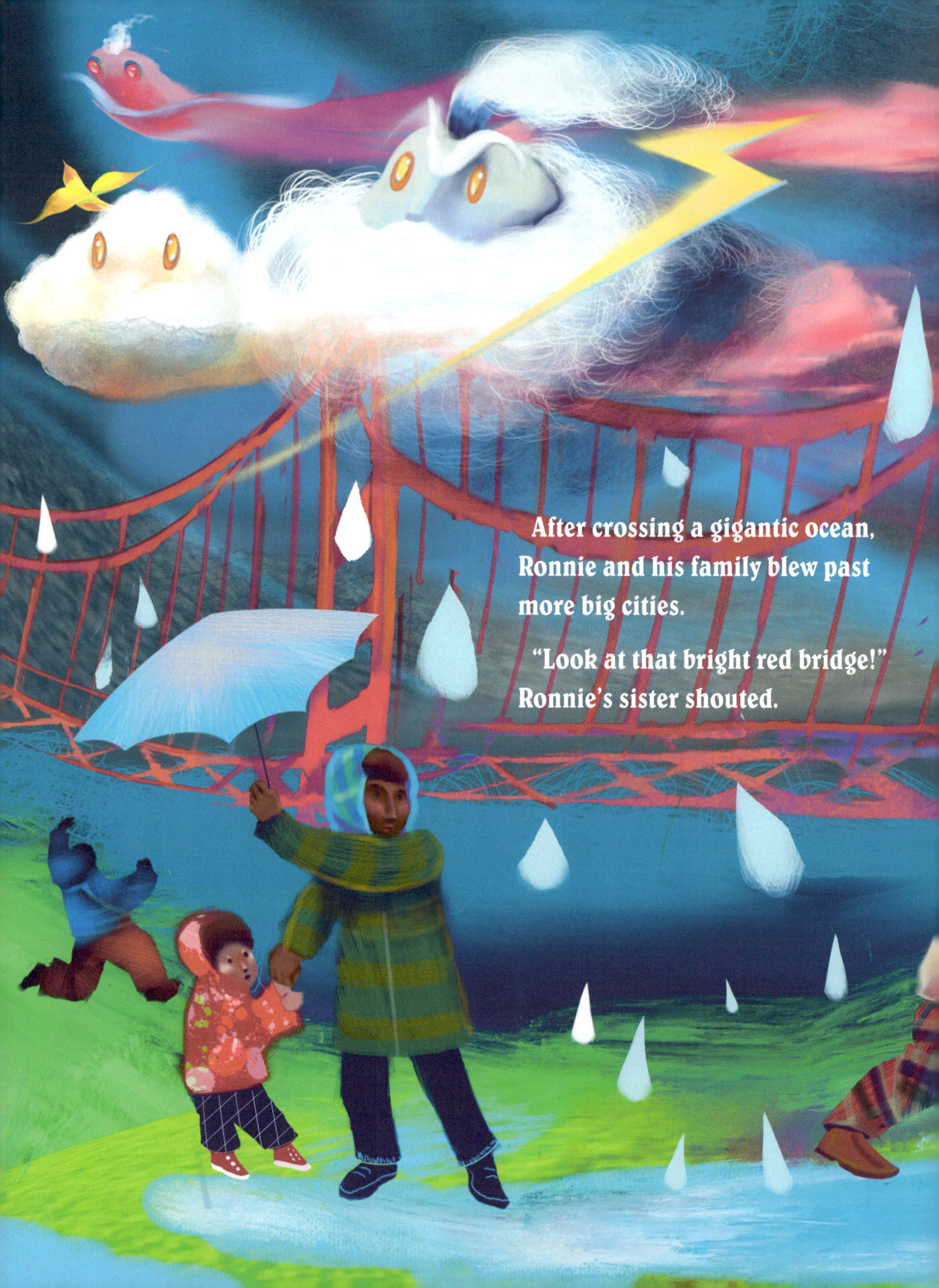

After crossing a gigantic ocean, Ronnie and his family blew past more big cities.

"Look at that bright red bridge!" Ronnie's sister shouted.

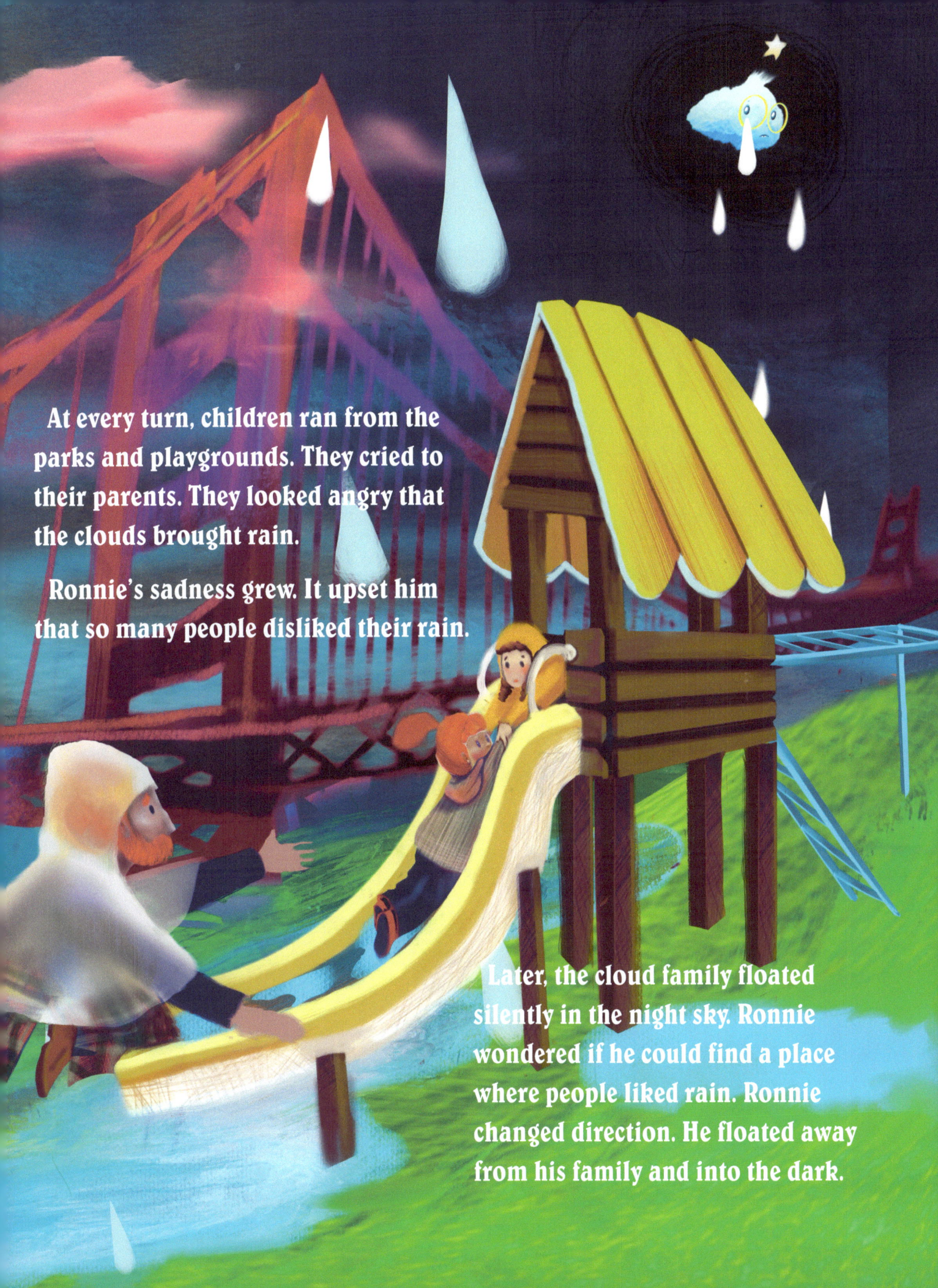

At every turn, children ran from the parks and playgrounds. They cried to their parents. They looked angry that the clouds brought rain.

Ronnie's sadness grew. It upset him that so many people disliked their rain.

Later, the cloud family floated silently in the night sky. Ronnie wondered if he could find a place where people liked rain. Ronnie changed direction. He floated away from his family and into the dark.

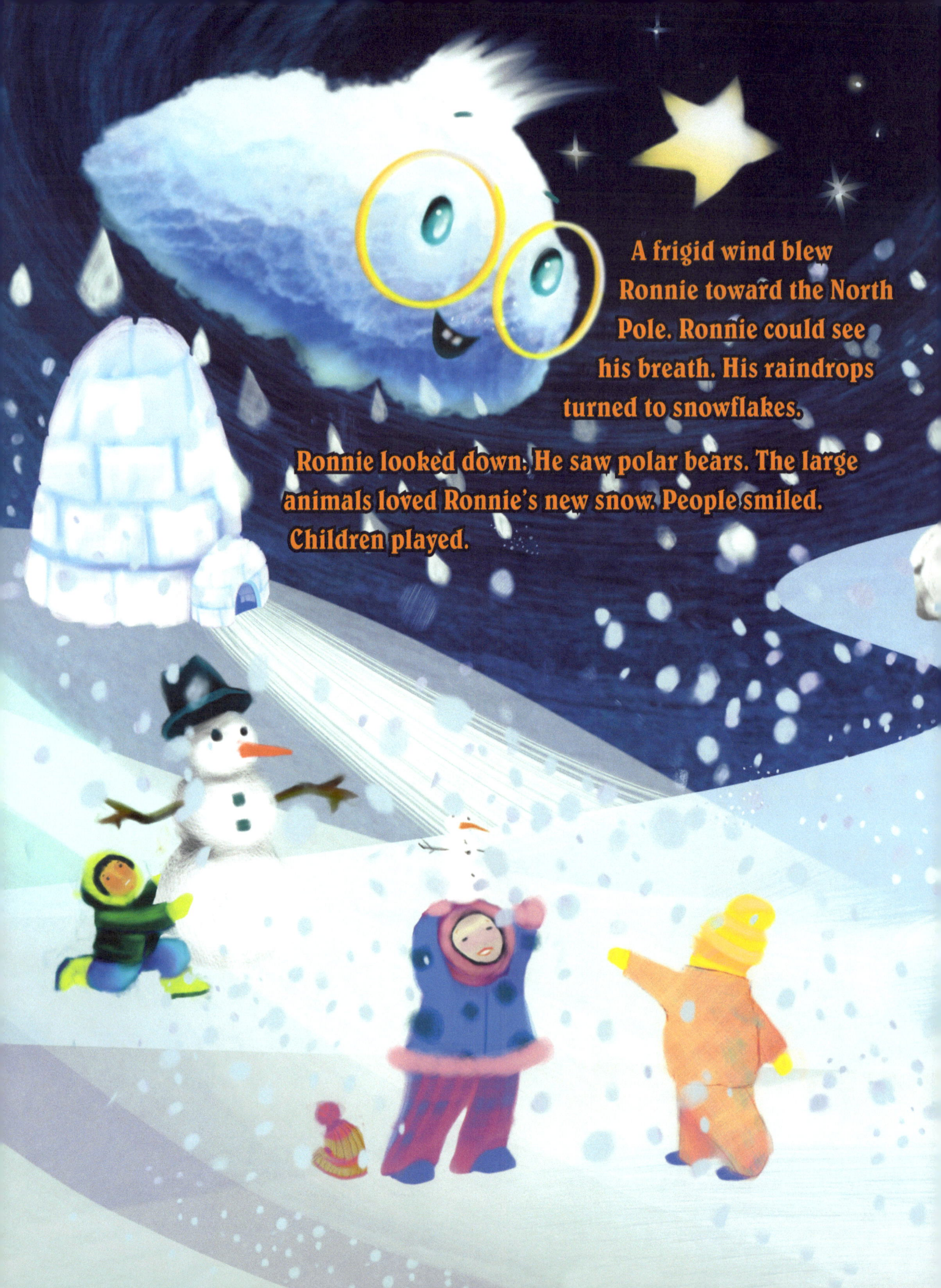

A frigid wind blew Ronnie toward the North Pole. Ronnie could see his breath. His raindrops turned to snowflakes.

Ronnie looked down. He saw polar bears. The large animals loved Ronnie's new snow. People smiled. Children played.

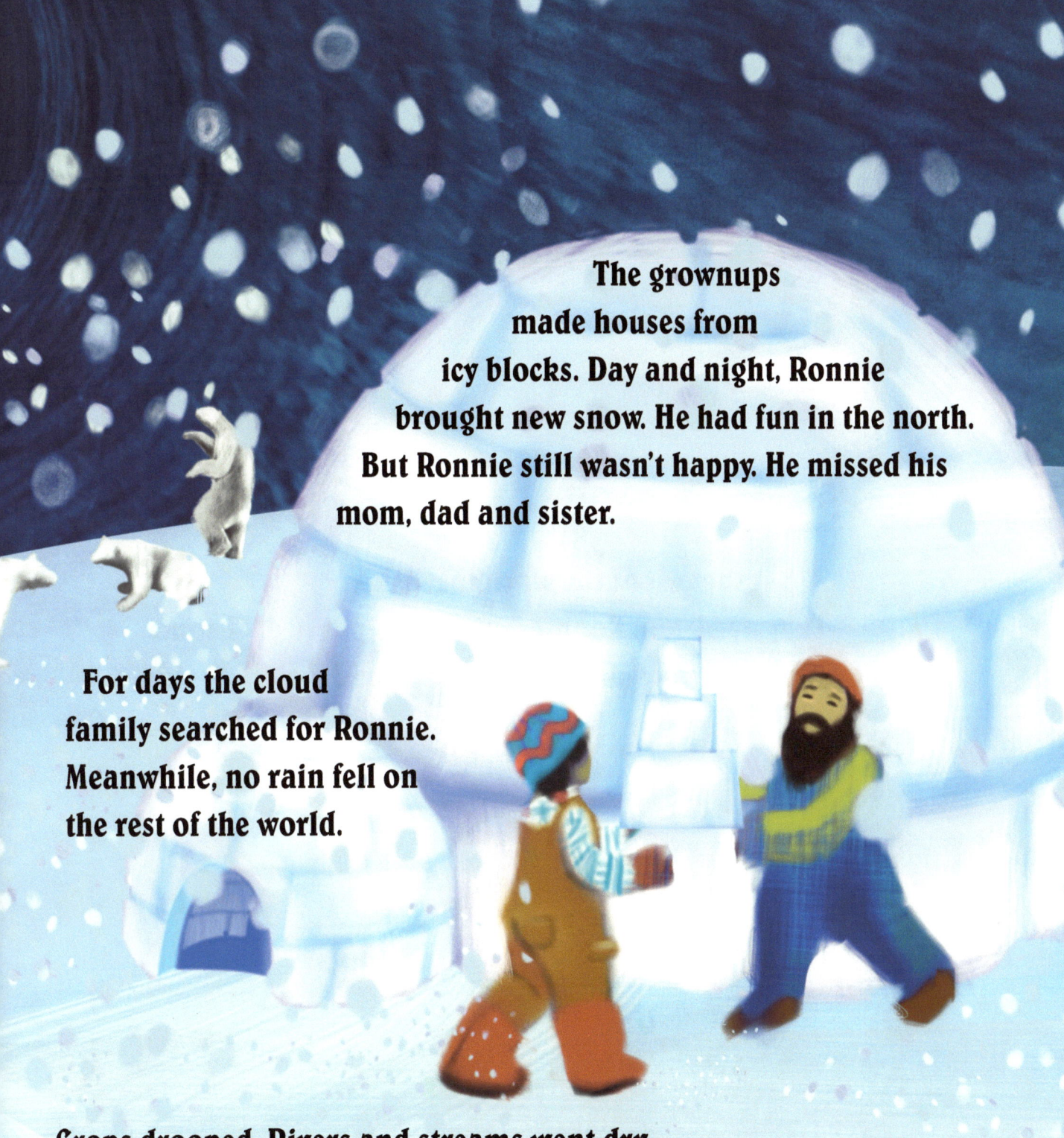

The grownups made houses from icy blocks. Day and night, Ronnie brought new snow. He had fun in the north. But Ronnie still wasn't happy. He missed his mom, dad and sister.

For days the cloud family searched for Ronnie. Meanwhile, no rain fell on the rest of the world.

Crops drooped. Rivers and streams went dry.

Finally, his family found Ronnie at the North Pole. His father roared with joy! "Ronnie, have you been here the whole time?"

"Yes, Dad. I came here because no one wants to see rain clouds," Ronnie replied. "Here they love snow clouds. So, I stayed."

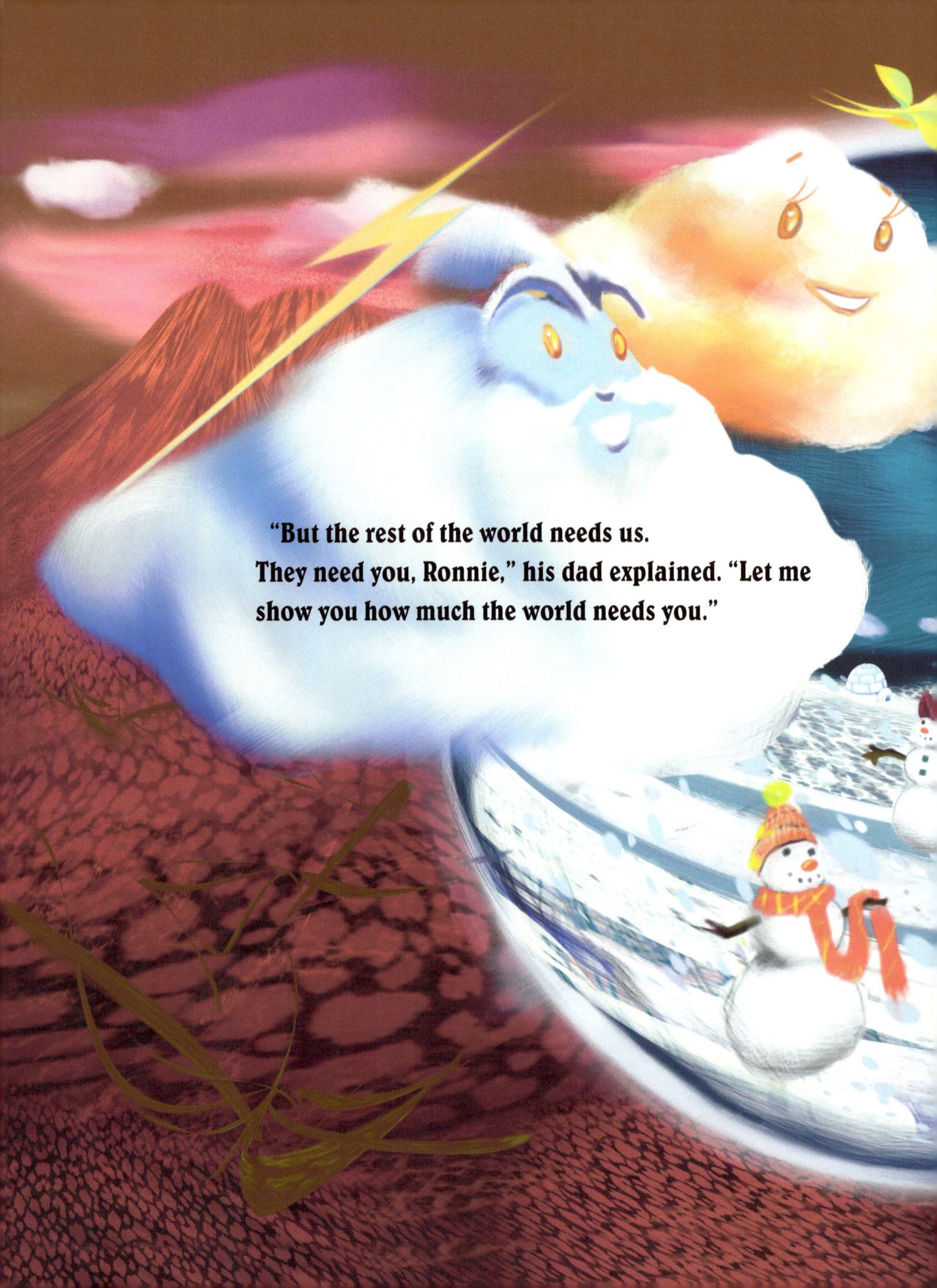

"But the rest of the world needs us.
They need you, Ronnie," his dad explained. "Let me
show you how much the world needs you."

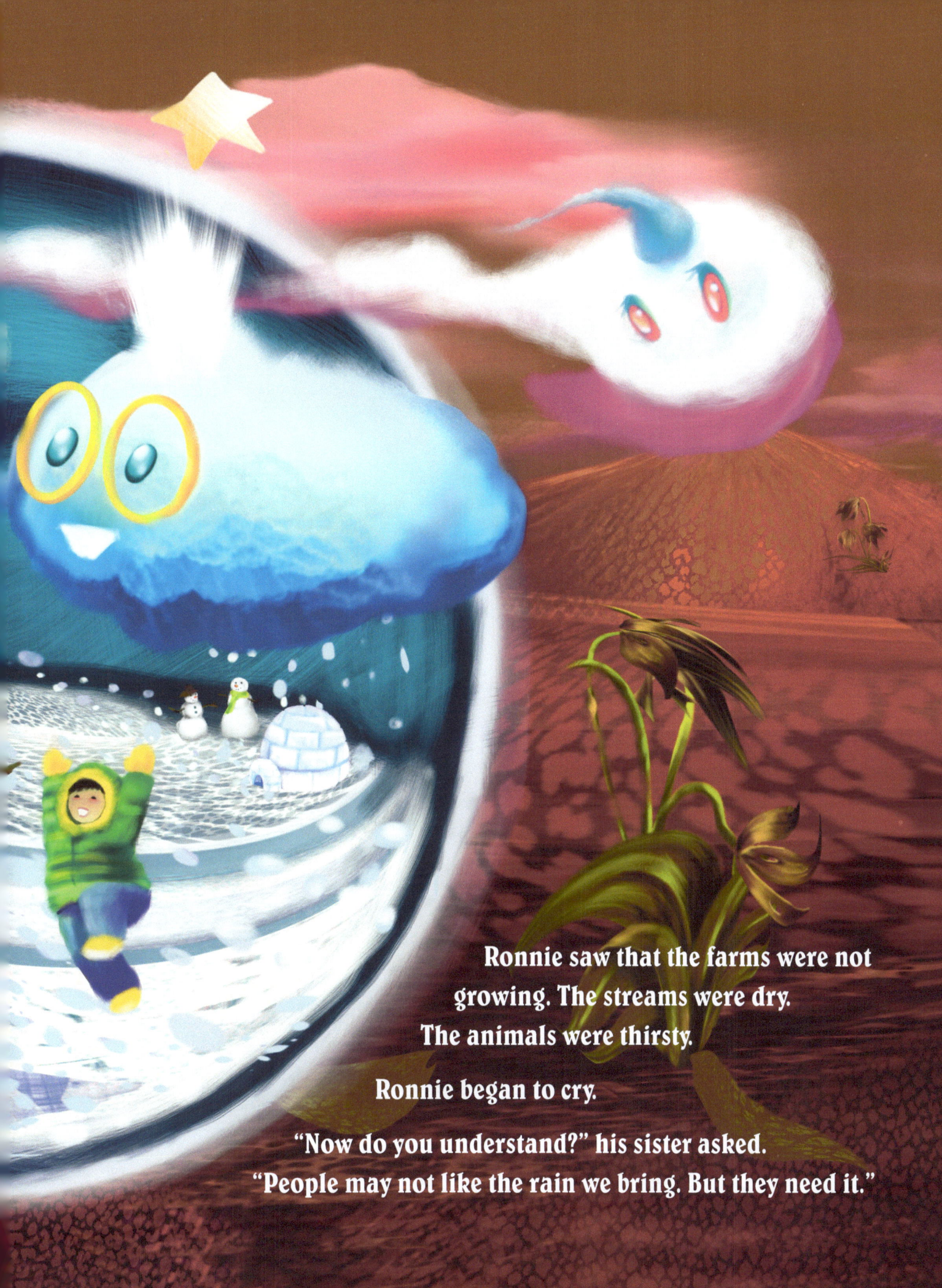

Ronnie saw that the farms were not growing. The streams were dry. The animals were thirsty.

Ronnie began to cry.

"Now do you understand?" his sister asked. "People may not like the rain we bring. But they need it."

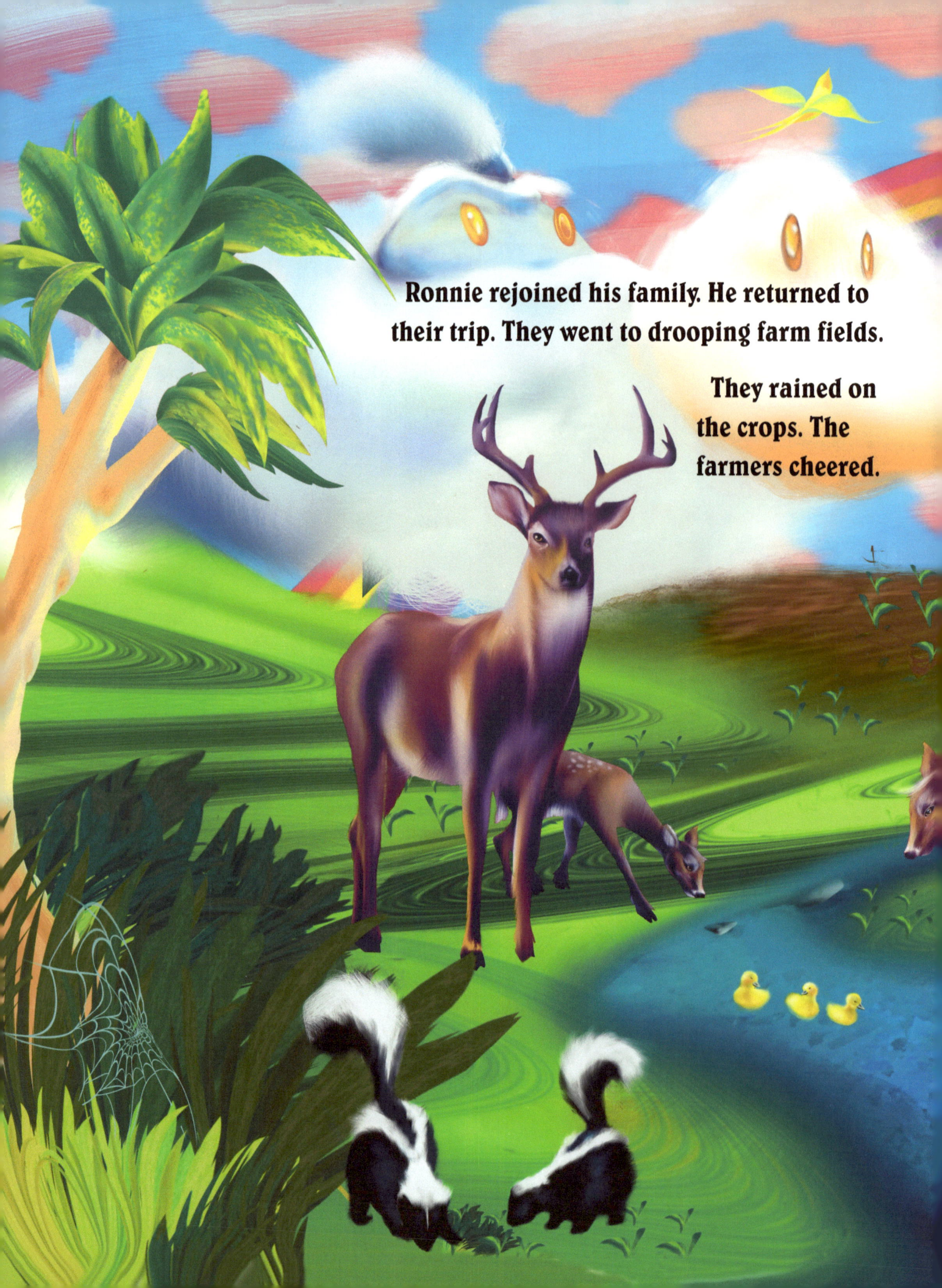

Ronnie rejoined his family. He returned to their trip. They went to drooping farm fields.

They rained on the crops. The farmers cheered.

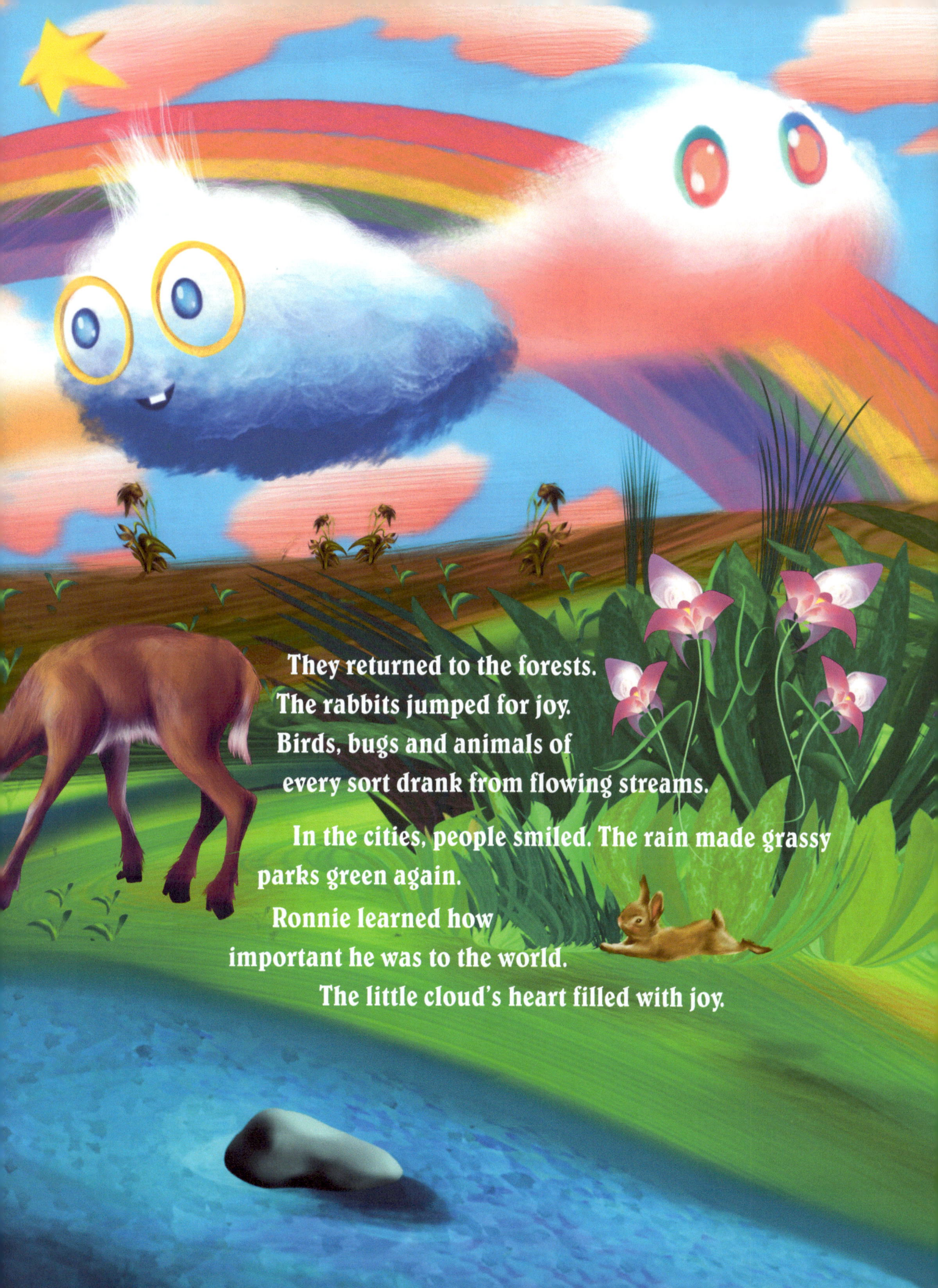

They returned to the forests.
The rabbits jumped for joy.
Birds, bugs and animals of
every sort drank from flowing streams.

In the cities, people smiled. The rain made grassy
parks green again.

Ronnie learned how
important he was to the world.
The little cloud's heart filled with joy.

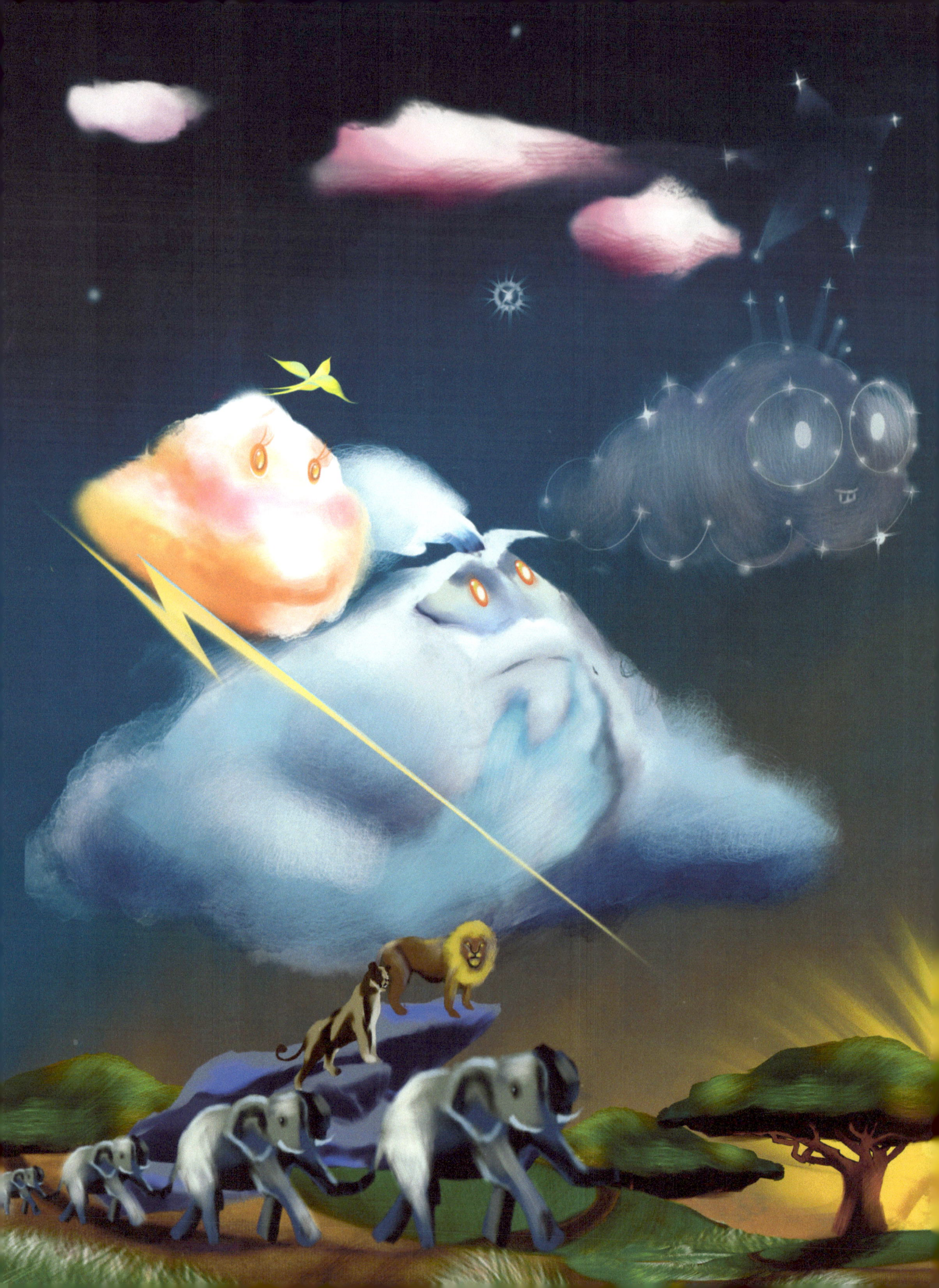

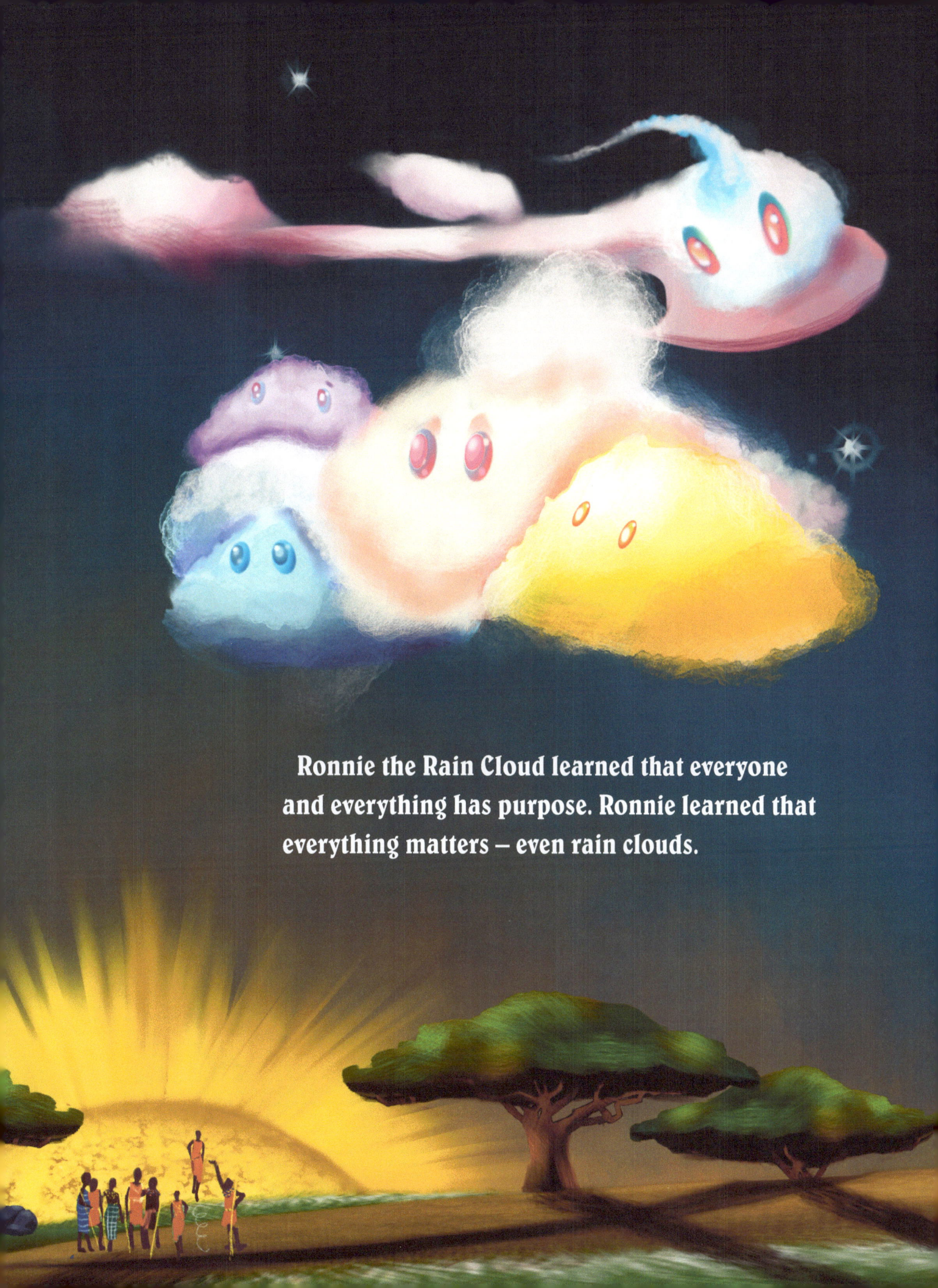

Ronnie the Rain Cloud learned that everyone and everything has purpose. Ronnie learned that everything matters – even rain clouds.

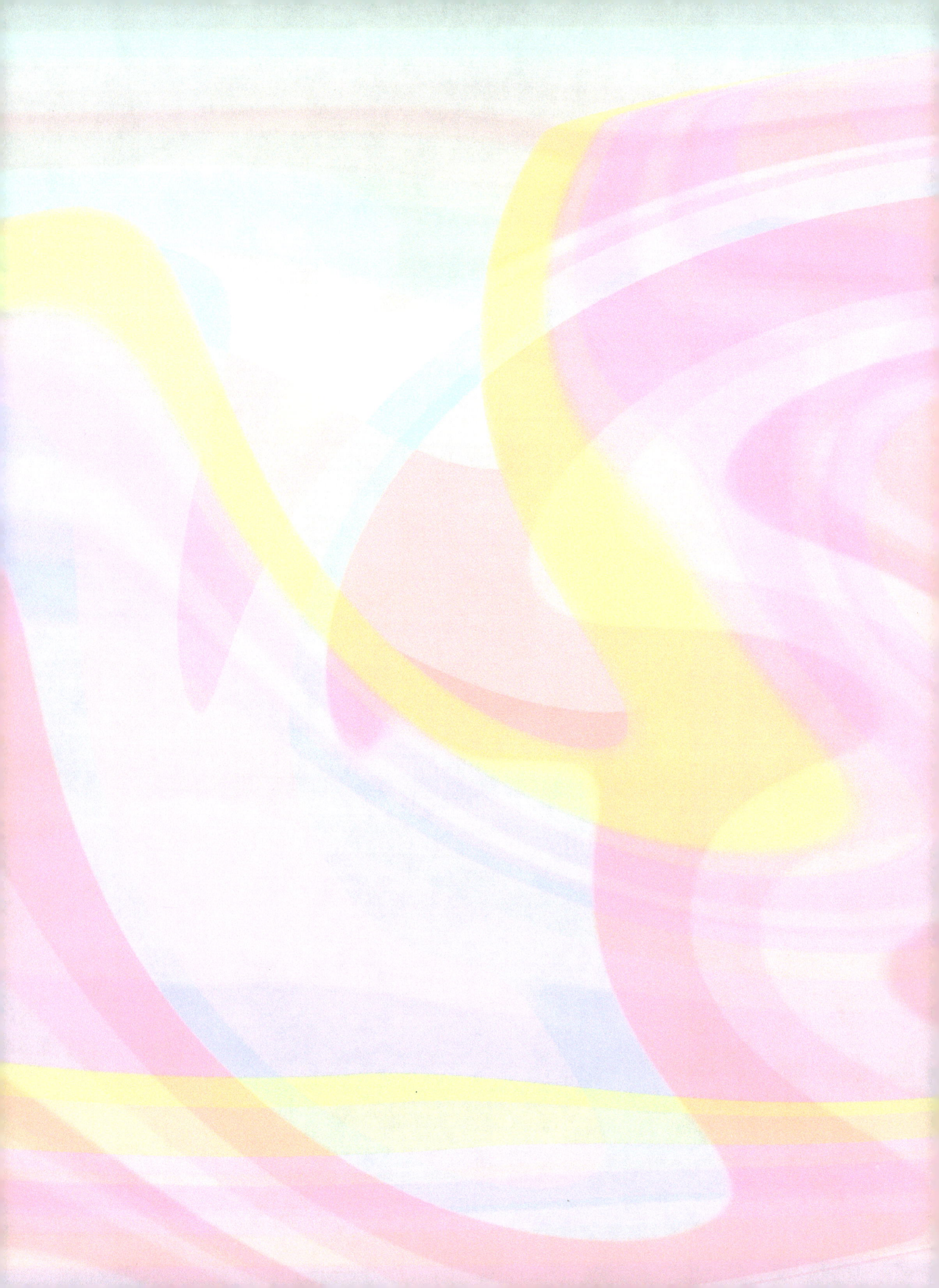